14/3/94			
1/11/94			

Pesticides and Fertilizers in Farming

Design: David West
Children's Book Design.
Editor: Roger Vlitos
Editorial Planning: Clark Robinson Ltd.
Picture Research: Cecilia Weston-Baker
Photographic Credits:
Cover and pages 12 left, 13 bottom, 16, 17 bottom, 19 right, 21 bottom left and 23 bottom: J. Allan Cash Library; pages 4, 6, 7 all, 8, 15, 18 right and 19 top, 20, 23 top, 25, 27 all and 29: Holt Studios; pages 10 and 11: Mary Evans Picture Library; page 13 top: Ardea; page 14: Shell Photographic Services; page 17 top and 29: Robert Harding Library; page 18 left: Science Photo Library; page 21 top: Bruce Coleman Ltd; page 23 top: Zefa; page 23 middle: Roger Vlitos.

Created and designed by
Aladdin Books Ltd
70 Old Compton Street
London W1V 5PA

A CIP catalogue record for this book
is available from the British Library

Printed in Belgium

First published in Great Britain in 1990 by
Gloucester Press
96 Leonard Street
London EC2A 4RH

ISBN 0-7496-0126-4

The publishers would like to acknowledge that the photographs reproduced within this book have been posed by models or have been obtained from photographic agencies.

Facts on

Pesticides and Fertilizers in Farming

Ron Taylor

GLOUCESTER PRESS
London · New York · Toronto · Sydney

CONTENTS

INTRODUCTION

The question of pesticides and fertilizers in farming is clouded by different shades of green.

The Green Revolution has doubled world food production since 1950. Much of this increase has been due to the widespread use of pesticides and manufactured fertilizers. Our ability to feed ourselves now rests on these chemical props.

The Green Movement maintains that most pesticides are poisons, and that we have succeeded in poisoning the food chains of the planet. The massive use of fertilizers has caused pollution in our rivers and seas.

Both points of view are basically correct. Finding a workable solution will not be easy. In global terms these chemical additives are like dangerous addictive drugs. We need them on a daily basis, but they are slowly killing us.

WHAT ARE PESTS?

Pests are living organisms that threaten human existence. Through their activities they can bring disease, famine, death and destruction. Parasites can feed on our blood or the nutrients we consume, and stored food is attacked by mould. Weeds choke our fields, and swarms of insects devour our crops.

In biological terms, pest species are very successful; they have adapted to living alongside people. In general, pests are small, difficult to kill, and under the right conditions they reproduce very rapidly.

Agricultural production has so far managed to keep pace with human population growth. But countries like the United States still lose about 40 per cent of their production to pests. In developing countries the losses are even greater. Unless we keep pests under control, they can have a great effect on food production.

DAMAGE TO STORES

Human food is especially at risk when collected for storage. In the United States, over 20 per cent of pest damage occurs after harvest. Throughout human history, rats and mice have posed a major threat to the stored food in warehouses and granaries. Nature has equipped these rodents to be excellent scavengers.

CRAWLING & FLYING

There are more than a million named species of insect, with many species still undiscovered. But a mere 100 species account for 90 per cent of all insect damage. Many of these are beetles and moths in their adult form, although it is often their young, called larvae, that are most destructive, feeding as caterpillars on leaves and as grubs in the soil. The locust is still the top insect enemy in hot, dry countries. Swarms of over 40 billion insects can occur, flying hundreds of kilometres in search of food. Such a swarm consumes about 80,000 tonnes of food a day. That's enough to keep 400,000 people alive for a year.

FIELD BATTLES

In the fields there is competition for space. For example, it is possible for a pair of poppies to deprive one wheat plant of life.

Tiny weevils, a type of beetle, feed by boring holes in the roots, stems and seeds of plants. Different species attack particular crops.

WHAT ARE PESTICIDES?

Pesticides are the substances we use to kill pests and prevent their spread. The main groups of pesticides are named for the type of pest they are aimed at – insecticides for insects, fungicides for fungi and herbicides for weeds. Most are poisons, and some contain similar ingredients to the nerve gas used in wars to kill people.

Within each group, scientists have tried to develop substances that are described as specific; they kill only pest species. Most pesticides are man-made chemicals, but some natural substances are also effective. Pyrethum, commonly used in household insect sprays, is obtained from a Kenyan wild flower. Pyrethum is lethal to wasps and flies, but is quite safe for humans. It is of limited use to farmers because rain can easily wash it off crops.

AERIAL SPRAYING

Where crops are grown in large fields or plantations, pesticides are often sprayed from the air. This process is very wasteful. Most of the spray is blown away by the wind, and only about 20 per cent lands on the target crops. Applying the pesticide from the ground would save on chemicals, but it would be very expensive in time and labour.

SWAMPS

Malaria is one of the main diseases still afflicting mankind. Each year it attacks millions of people in tropical countries. The disease is caused by a parasite which is passed to man by blood-sucking mosquitos. Part of the fight against malaria has involved spraying the swamps in which mosquitos breed with DDT and other insecticides. Since 1945, more than one billion people have been freed from the risks of malaria, and some seven million human lives have been saved thanks to insecticides.

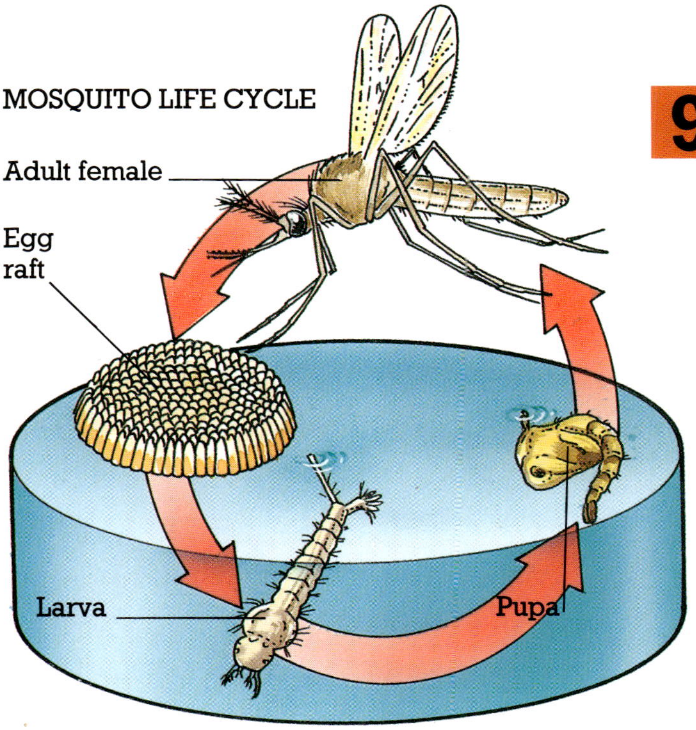

HOW MUCH ?

Developed countries use at least one kilogram of pesticide per person per year. In Africa and Asia, the amount may be 50 times less. In the United States farming accounts for 75 per cent of all usage, and weeds are the biggest target.

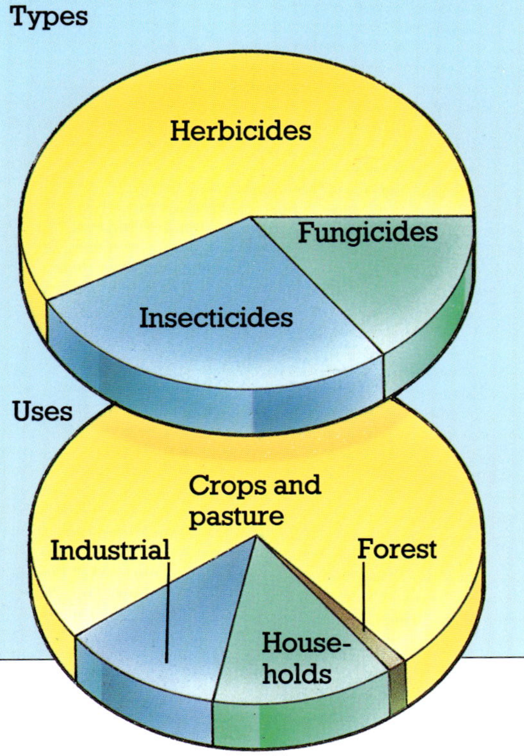

10 PLAGUES OF PESTS

Malaria is not the only disease caused by pests. In 1340 rats scuttled ashore from a ship in a Mediterranean port. Within ten years, more than one third of the population of Europe had died of bubonic plague. The rats brought with them the "Black Death". In the trenches of World War One, filthy and overcrowded conditions meant that soldiers became infested with parasitic lice. These lice carried the bacteria that cause the disease typhus, and an epidemic broke out killing hundreds of thousands. When it was introduced, DDT was hailed as a scientific wonder. It has since saved more human lives than any other man-made chemical. But studies have shown that DDT is not as safe as scientists first thought.

RATS AND PLAGUE

The Black Death was caused by a combination of three species. The bacteria that cause bubonic plague were carried by rat fleas. The rats invaded houses in search of food, and the fleas fed on human blood and left their eggs in people's clothes. Once established, bubonic plague spread from person to person.

FAMINE

Plant diseases can be equally devastating, especially when they attack essential food crops. During the 19th century, the Irish potato crop was destroyed several times by a fungus known as late blight. The worst outbreak was in 1845-6, when tens of thousands starved in a "potato famine" and many more decided to emigrate. Ireland still remembers the devastation and hardship.

DDT

What scientists at first missed was the fact that DDT accumulates in animal's bodies. As it travels up the food chain, the chemical becomes more concentrated. Eventually it reaches harmful levels, especially in predators.

Another surprise for the scientists was the fact that some pest species rapidly developed a resistance to DDT. The more DDT that was used, the more species became resistant to it. Today there are well over 400 pests which DDT will no longer kill.

Concentration of DDT in the food chain (ppm = parts per million)

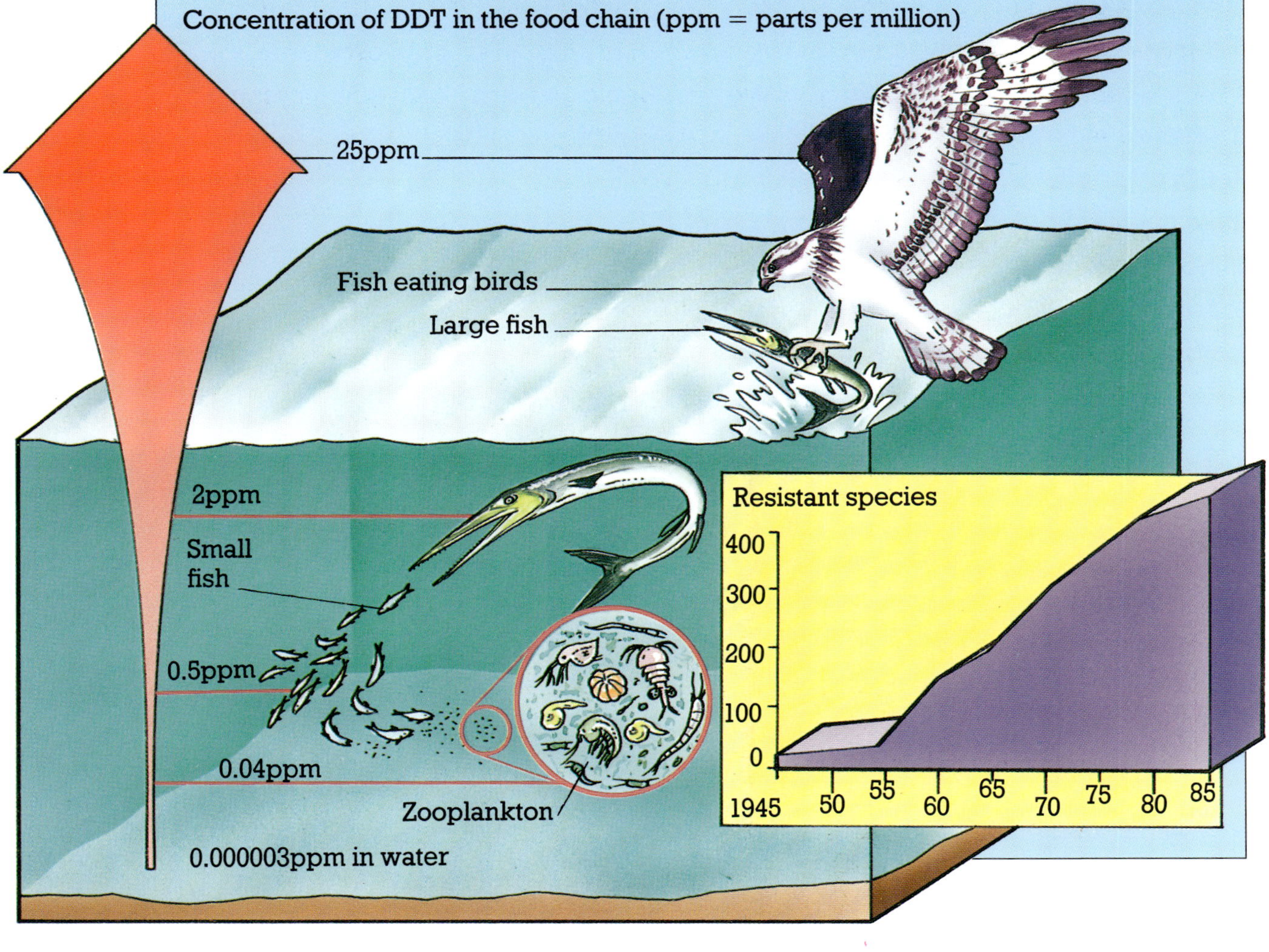

AGAINST PROPERTY

Most pests directly threaten our health or our food supplies, but some endanger other basic human needs. The cotton for our clothing can be eaten by weevils outdoors and by moth larvae in the wardrobe. Even the structure of our buildings is attacked. Many insects have evolved ways of digesting the tough cellulose fibres in plants. Some, like termites, make use of internal bacteria to do this. In the Tropics, termites can consume a whole fallen tree, and the timbers of a house are an attractive meal for other insects. The fast-growing water hyacinth clogs thousands of kilometres of waterways, and ships may carry an unwanted living load of barnacles and seaweed. Tiny plants and algae even grow inside oil tanks and contaminate the contents.

AGAINST COTTON

The prosperity of the southern United States once depended on a single crop, "King Cotton". The destruction caused by the arrival of the boll weevil, which feeds on cotton before it flowers, led to poverty for thousands. Although cotton is no longer "king", the control of this insect still accounts for 35 per cent of all pesticides used in the United States.

AGAINST WOOD

Termites are not the only insects to relish a diet of wood. Some species of wasp and beetle are considered pests for the damage they do to living trees as well as to timber products.

Deathwatch beetles and woodworm tunnel their living accommodation in furniture and rafters. Woodwasp larvae eat their way to adulthood inside a tree. This tunnelling activity can also spread epidemics such as Dutch Elm Disease.

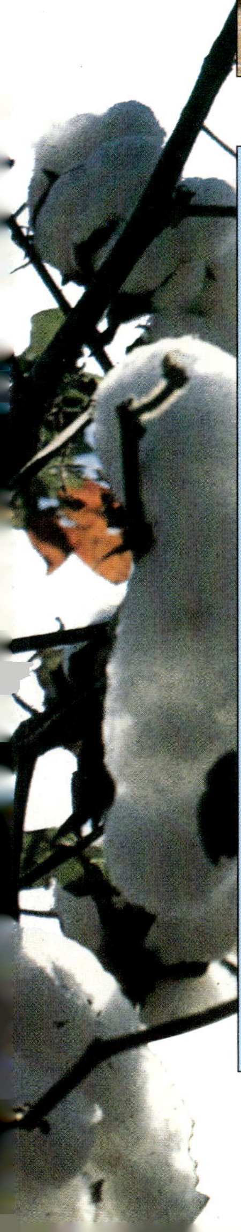

SEA ATTACK

Worms that could eat through a wooden ship are defeated by modern steel hulls, but they were once dreaded by mariners. Today they still burrow into piers and quays. More costly is the loss of speed caused by an accumulation of barnacles and seaweed on a ship's hull. Removal often means taking the vessel out of the water. Modern methods involve the use of anti-fouling paint which contains long-lasting chemicals that prevent marine growth. The chemicals slowly dissolve and become absorbed into food chains.

FIGHTING DISEASE CARRIERS

Disease carriers are often described as vectors. With malaria, mosquitos are the vector; with plague, it is rats and fleas. Recently, our understanding of disease vectors has increased considerably and many diseases are now under control, although other disease vectors continue to bring misery and death to millions.

Treating a disease in human patients with drugs is a very expensive form of control. Attacking the disease vectors is much more efficient, as with malaria, but not all vectors respond to simple attack with pesticides. There are difficulties in matching a poison to a particular vector, and scientists have to devise very specific chemicals. Applying a pesticide can also be a problem, especially if the pest lives in the water supply.

TSETSE FLY

Most of tropical Africa is infested with the tsetse fly which carries "sleeping sickness". Epidemics have killed up to half the human population in some areas. No special pesticide has yet been devised to deal with the tsetse fly, and spraying half a continent with DDT is neither safe nor practical.

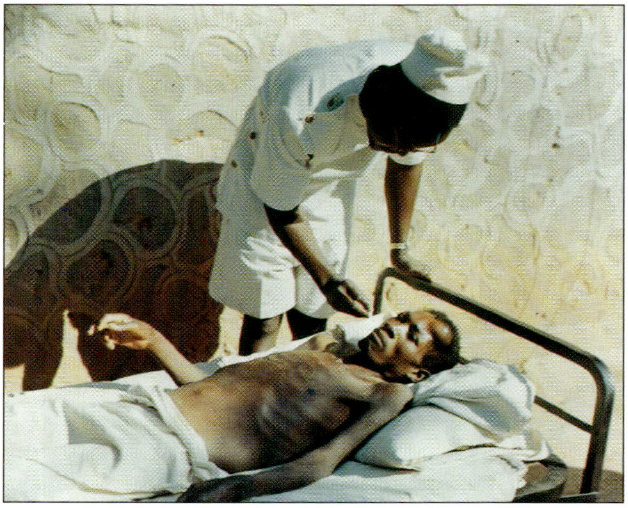

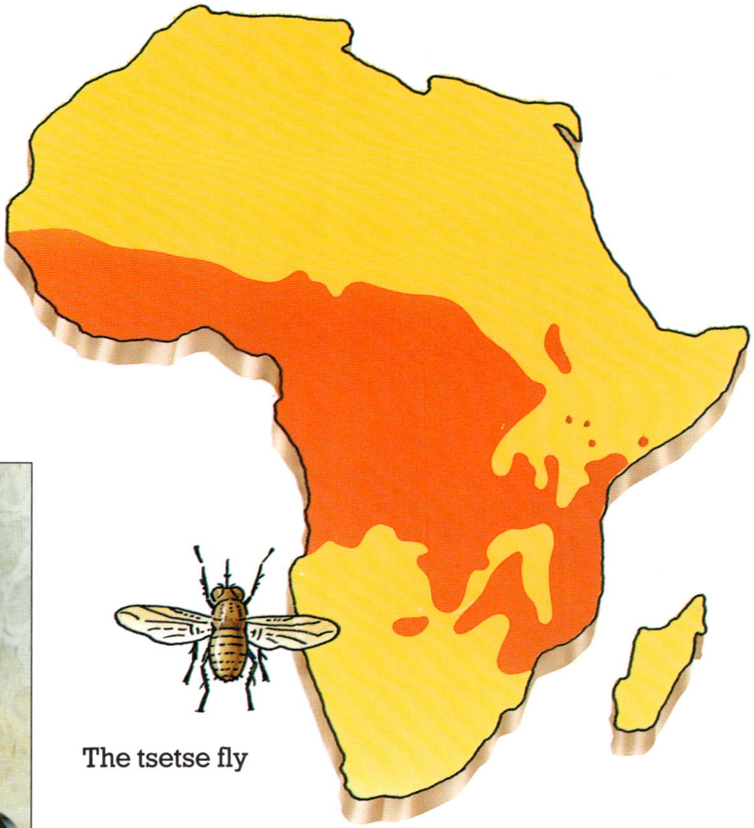

The tsetse fly

Present distribution

BILHARZIA

Bilharzia is a wasting disease that afflicts millions in poor tropical countries. The disease is caused by a tiny parasitic fluke that has a complicated life-cycle. The parasite develops inside freshwater snails. The larvae then burrow out in search of bigger hosts. Human skin provides little resistance to them, and people who work in irrigated fields are especially at risk. Inside the body, the parasite matures and lays eggs which are spread by human waste. The problem lies in deciding which stage of the cycle to attack.

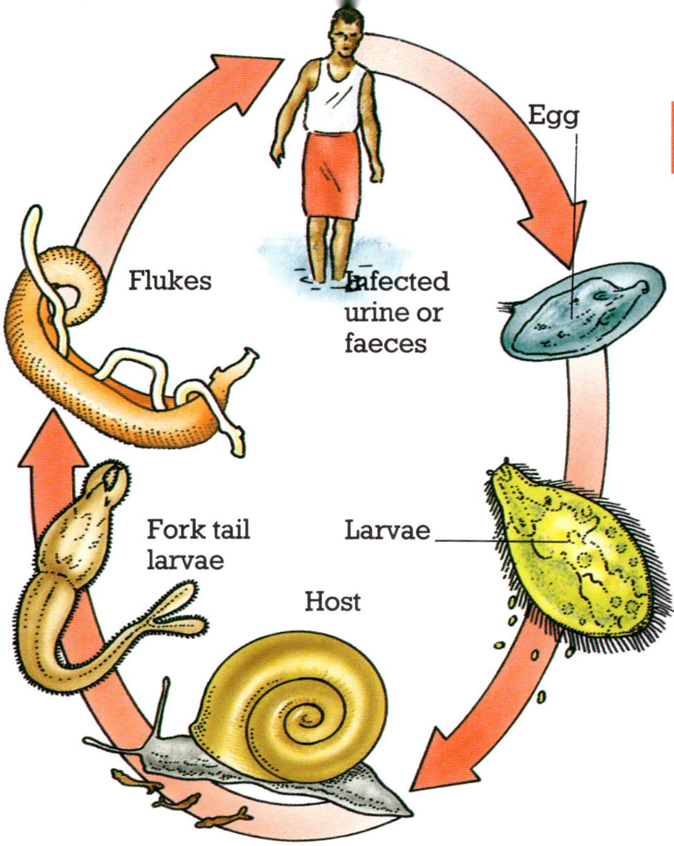

BUG-BUSTERS

Direct attack with powerful poisons is a sure way of killing insects. Such methods can be used in farming, but insecticides often destroy the useful insects (such as ladybirds) with the bad (such as aphids). Many insect species are beneficial, even essential, to our crops.

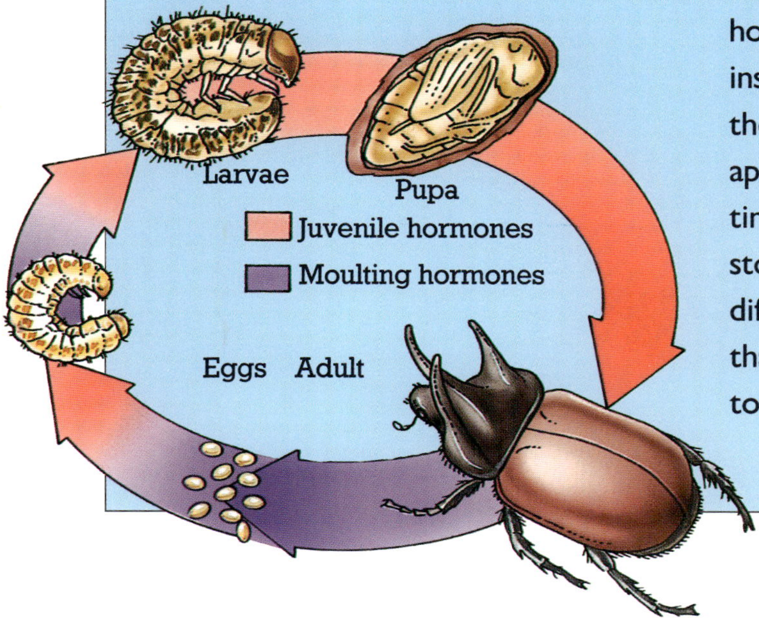

The most modern pesticides use hormones. The various stages of an insect's life-cycle are triggered by the release of such chemicals. By applying these at carefully selected times further development can be stopped. Different species use different hormones, which means that insecticides can be tailor-made to deal with specific pests.

WAR ON WEEDS

Weeds are the plants that man does not want. The conditions we create to encourage our crops are highly attractive to other species. Some weeds have almost become domesticated. These "habitation weeds" are the natural companions of our food crops. Each weed occupies valuable space, takes nutrients and moisture from the soil, and may create unwanted shade. Some bind themselves around other plants and literally strangle our food. Others are poisonous to our livestock, but these poisons are part of the plant's natural defences, and are used to combat their own enemies. Weed control is probably the biggest single problem in world agriculture. Chemical herbicides save countless hours of back-breaking labour, because weeding is very difficult to do with machines.

THE WEED

Couch grass, docks, thistles and nettles are some of the most persistent and troublesome weeds, to gardeners and farmers alike. Ragwort and charlock in meadows can cause illness in cattle. In the USA, poison-ivy makes some land almost uninhabitable. In Australia, the prickly pear cactus infests thousands of square kilometres.

WEEDING

In the garden, weeding means hours of hard work. For the crop farmer, hand-weeding would mean an impossible amount of labour. The introduction of selective herbicides, which kill certain plants but not others, has transformed agriculture. Some of the chemical weed-killers act on exposed surfaces, and are especially useful against broad-leaved weeds such as dock. Others are absorbed into the weeds from the soil. The most sophisticated herbicides use hormones to make the weed grow too quickly so that it collapses and dies.

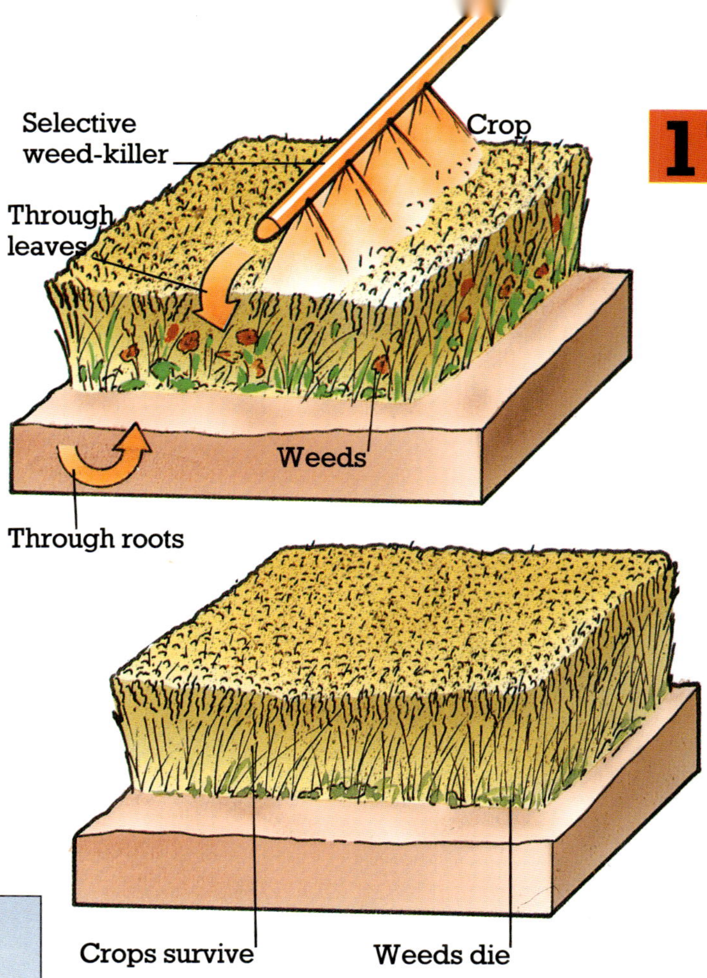

FUNGI AND MOULDS

Fungi are one of the major causes of plant disease. Root crops such as potatoes are not the only ones affected. Fields of wheat may be turned black by smut fungi, or red by rust fungi. The honey fungus will eventually kill the tree on which it grows. Ripe fruit, stored food, and even clothing and carpets, are all liable to be attacked by mould and mildew. These types of fungi are part of the natural processes of decay by which nutrients are recycled. They also cause hundreds of millions of pounds worth of damage. Some fungi also cause disease in animals and people. The strange life-cycle of fungi makes them difficult to combat with chemicals. Fungi attack surfaces, so the whole of the item to be treated must be covered with a fungicide.

WHAT THEY ARE

All fungi grow as tiny, hollow threads (hyphae) arranged in a network (mycelium). Normally, they live in the ground. Some pest species invade plants through the roots. They extend their network into the structure of the plant, eventually killing it. Visible fungi, such as mushrooms, grow out of the mycelium as fruiting bodies.

REPRODUCTION

The fruiting bodies contain large numbers of sporangia, and fungi which do not produce fruiting bodies may carry their sporangia on stalks. Sporangia contain spores and there are often millions of these. The air we breathe is full of spores from common fungi such as the Penicillium mould which grows on bread. Each one of these can start a new mycelium wherever it lands.

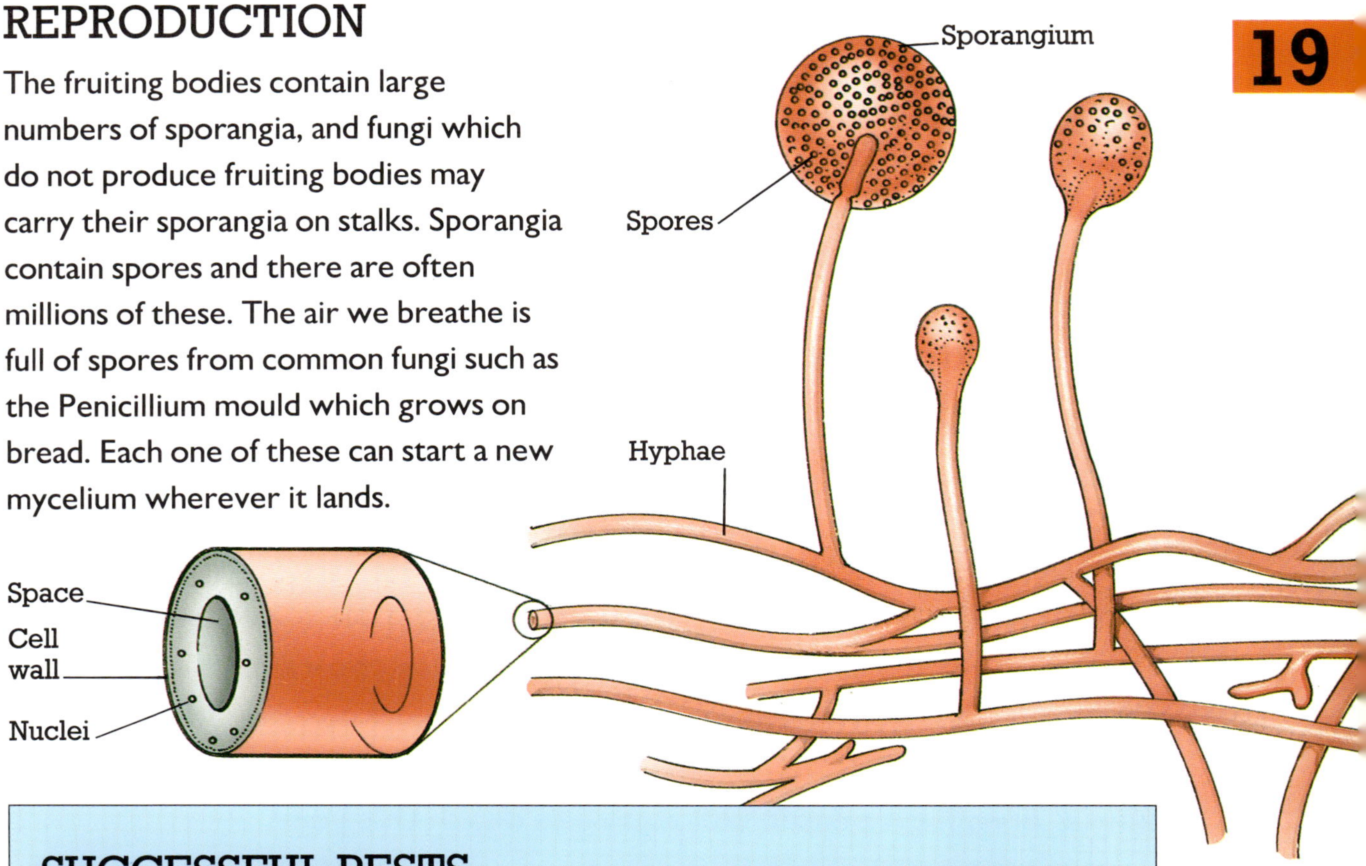

SUCCESSFUL PESTS

Smut fungi attack all parts of a cereal plant, especially the grain. The infection is not noticeable until spores are produced. By then it is too late and the damage has been done.

Wet and dry rot are the names we give the fungi that attack and cause decay in our buildings. Timbers and floorboards can become so infested with the threads of mycelium that they crumble at a touch.

PESTICIDE PROBLEMS

Pesticides have brought tremendous benefits to mankind. We rely on them to preserve our health and to keep our food supplies intact. But there has been a price which we are only now having to face. Scientists have always been aware that pesticides presented a problem to wildlife, but they underestimated the risk. In part they overlooked the effects of concentration in food chains. They also failed to appreciate just how wastefully the new pesticides would be applied. Nature cannot tolerate much more man-made poison. Restricting the use of pesticides is not an easy choice to make. Throughout the world there are problems with food production and distribution. One in seven of us is accustomed to hunger, and about 20 million people will starve to death this year.

MONOCULTURE

Half of the world's food comes from just three crops – wheat, rice and maize. The large-scale cultivation of cereals requires that huge areas of land have to be farmed as a monoculture.

Such methods are a tremendous gamble. If just one plant disease manages to penetrate our pesticide defences, the results could be catastrophic. We are absolutely dependent on pesticides as long as we have single-crop economies.

THREAT TO WILDLIFE

Most pesticides are fairly harmless in low concentrations. But the very factors that make them so useful also enable them to become more concentrated. A good pesticide is one that lasts a long time and does not break down chemically. These qualities enable them to enter food chains, so causing harm to wildlife. For example, birds that eat insects sprayed with pesticide lay eggs with weakened shells. The effects of DDT were noticed quickly, and it is now banned in the USA and Europe.

THE HUMAN FACTOR

Protective clothing worn while applying pesticides has become normal practice in some countries. In others, unprotected workers face exposure to dangerous chemicals.

There is now considerable concern about pesticides entering human food chains. Many crops are sprayed with fungicide after harvest so that they remain fresh for the shops.

USING NATURAL ENEMIES

Nature exercises very subtle control over a species' population. The two main factors are the availability of food and the size of the populations that feed upon it. An increase of food leads to an increase in numbers. In turn this represents more food for the predators. Human activity, especially agriculture, increases the amount of food available for pest species. By increasing the populations of species that prey on the pests, we can sometimes use nature herself against them. The process is not easy. Often, a particular pest may have been introduced to an area by man himself. There may be no natural predators in the region. In some cases, foreign predators have been introduced to control a pest.

A FOOD WEB

Food chains interconnect with others to form a complex network called a "food web". By increasing the population of one species, we can affect the population of other species throughout the web.

Plants (the primary producers) are at one end. In the middle are the plant-eating animals (the primary consumers). At the other end are the carnivores (the secondary consumers).

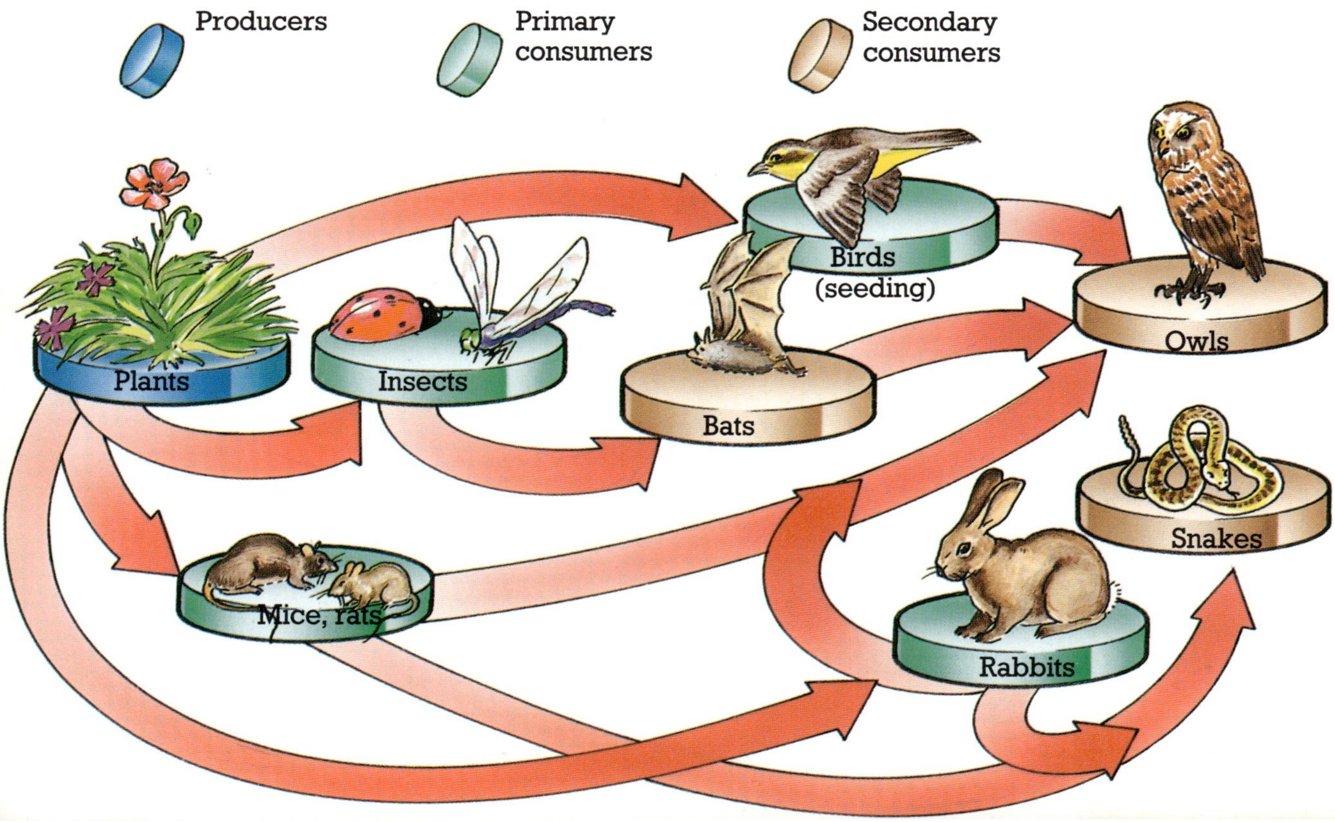

INTO PRACTICE

Both insects and predators can be used as natural controls. Ladybirds have been used successfully to combat aphids that can cause large-scale crop destruction.

Large populations of predators can be bred quickly to overcome unwanted pests. European predators have been introduced into North America to deal with insect pests in coniferous forests.

In Malaysia, palm-oil is the most important export commodity and millions of pounds worth of damage is caused by rats in the palm plantations. In some areas, the introduction of barn owls has had a dramatic effect in the decrease of the number of rats.

NATURAL FERTILIZERS

Fertilizers are a means of supplying additional nutrients and minerals to soil. In nature, these substances are produced by the decay of animal and vegetable material. A natural ecosystem produces enough humus to sustain itself. Humus is a mixture of partly decomposed natural material found in topsoil. It helps to retain water and nutrients for plant roots. Man's crops take much more out of the soil than natural vegetation. If the same crop is grown repeatedly, the soil will become exhausted and useless. Some crops, such as clover, help put nutrients back into the soil. In order to keep the soil fertile, different crops can be rotated from field to field. When animals are allowed to graze in fields that are "resting" their dung also acts as fertilizer. Plants can also be allowed to decay to form compost.

HOW IT WORKS

Decay releases the nutrients stored in living organisms. The uppermost layer of soil is called topsoil. This is composed largely of decaying vegetation (humus) and is perfect for seedlings and the healthy growth of plants.

The nutrients are slowly released into the soil where they can be tapped by roots. Earthworms and other soil dwellers also help to mix the humus into the rest of the soil. Some minerals rise up from the underlying rock.

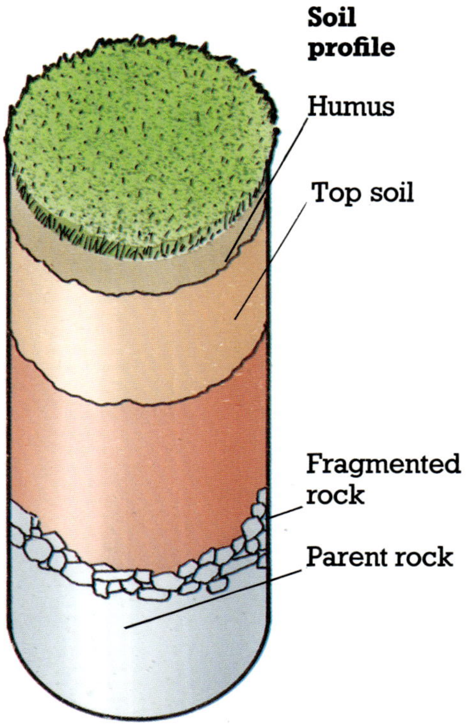

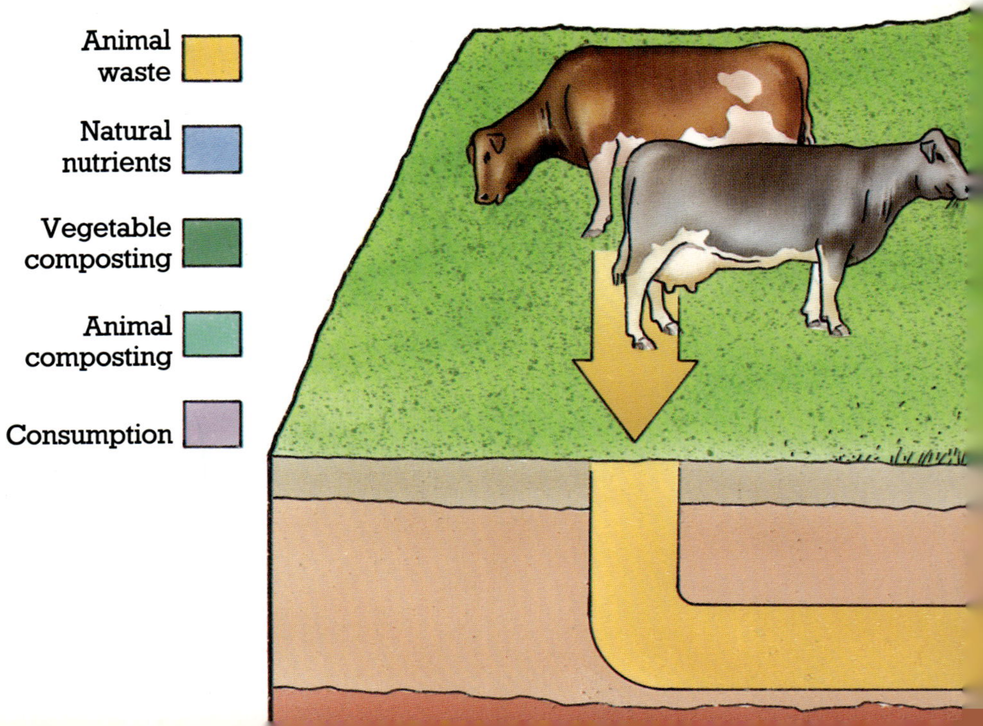

CROP ROTATION

Traditional "slash and burn" farming can force a good crop out of poor soil. But the land must be left to recover for at least 15 years. Modern methods of crop rotation usually work on a four year cycle. Plants such as clover help to "fix" the essential element nitrogen into the soil. This system is most efficient when crops and animals are farmed together. Such a system is called mixed farming.

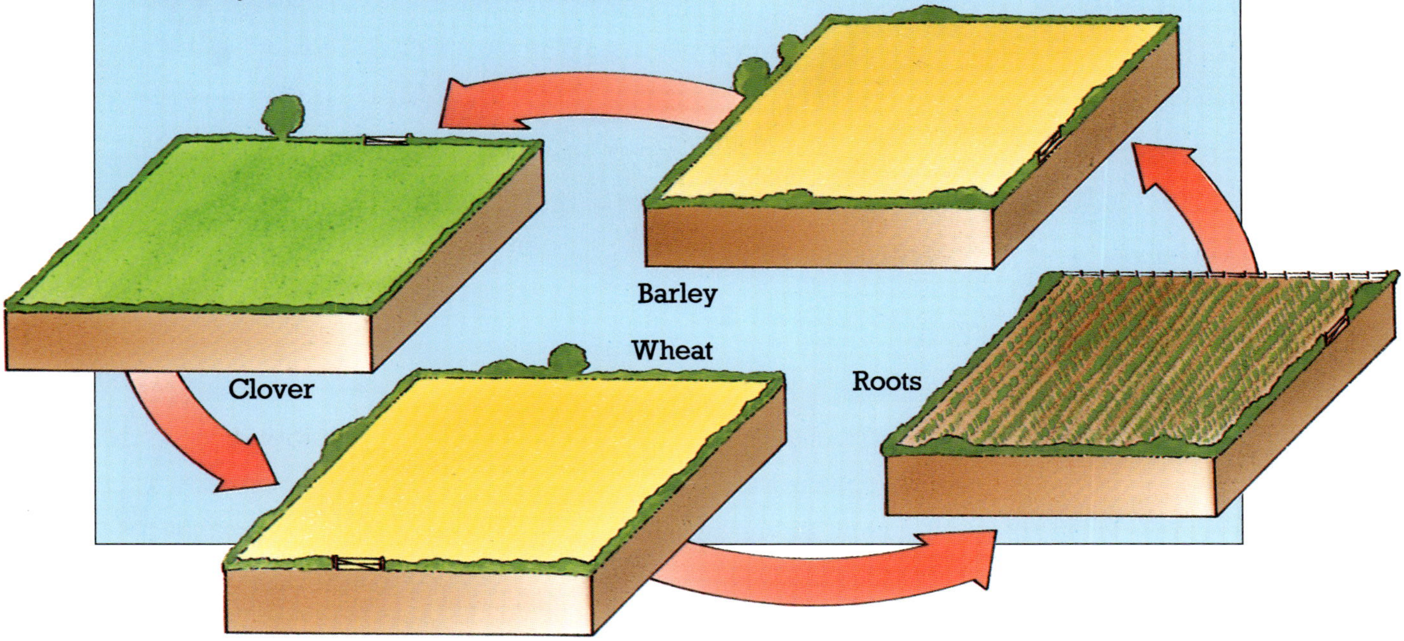

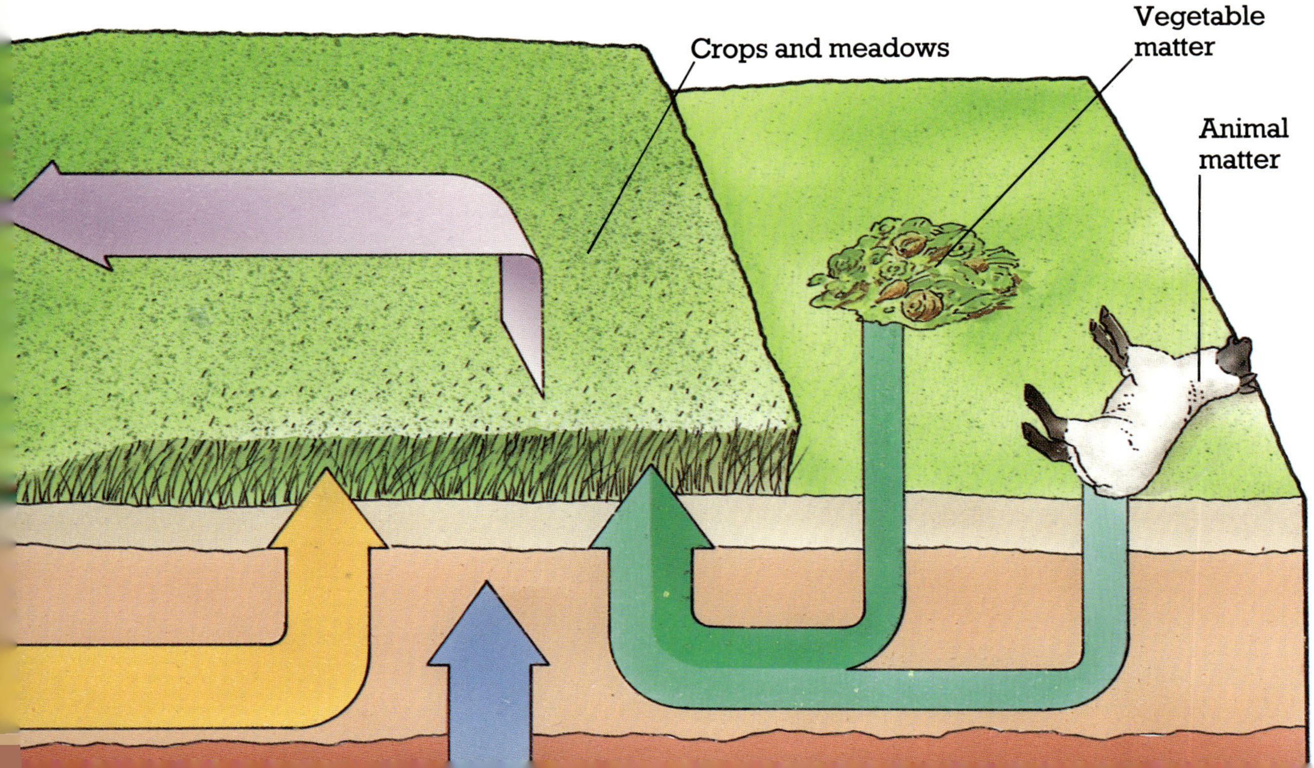

ARTIFICIAL FERTILIZERS

Cutting down trees and burning them before planting a crop is the oldest method of farming we have. Called "slash and burn", this method produces some fertilizer from the ash, although it is a short-term solution and destroys valuable forests. Other traditional soil additives include fish-meal, powdered bone and dried blood, but these were never available for large-scale use. In our time we have perfected the mass-production of artificial nitrate fertilizers. More than any other single invention, artificial fertilizers have transformed modern agriculture. Farmers can now grow the same crop in the same field year after year. In developed countries, artificial fertilizers have led to record harvests. In some developing countries they have helped double food production. Between 1950 and 1980 the consumption of artificial fertilizers rose 800 per cent.

THE NEED FOR THEM

No plant can live solely on sunlight and water. Many vital substances must be absorbed from the soil. As man makes greater demands on his land in terms of productivity, so the crops make greater demands on the soil.

Modern high-yield varieties can extract as much as 80 per cent of the available nitrogen. Most of the nutrients leave the field with the crop. We are already farming most of the suitable land and we need fertilizers to maintain production at the present rate.

Crops use up nutrients when growing.

Harvesting removes them from the field.

SPREADING

Fertilizers are applied in huge quantities. Wheat may require up to 500 kg per hectare. Machines are ideal for spreading fertilizer, but there is inevitable waste as spillage and rain disperse the products meant for the crop. Fertilizers are also sprayed onto grazing land. Letters indicate that the fertilizer contains nitrogen (N) phosphorus (P) and potassium (K).

Next year's crop depends on fertilizers.

FAULTY FERTILIZERS

Crops do not use all the fertilizer we apply. The surplus does not stay in the soil, it is washed out by the rain. This rainwater is described as agricultural run-off. Fertilizer that enters the water supply creates both long and short-term problems. The nutrients in agricultural run-off provide a rich source of food for microscopic algae that live in ponds and streams. These organisms reproduce very quickly until they have used up the available food. When the algae die off, the process of decomposition removes all the oxygen from the water. As a result all the other water-life suffocates, and the entire body of water becomes lifeless. Fertilizers are a major cause of water pollution, and the problem is now spreading to the seas.

NITRATE TIME-BOMB

Nitrates from fertilizer are now found in our tap water. Some scientists have linked these pollutants with cancer and other diseases in humans. The evidence is not conclusive, and at present nitrate levels in drinking water are fairly low. Some experts believe that most of the nitrates have not yet reached our water reserves, and that we are sitting on a pollution time-bomb.

SLURRY

Artificial fertilizers are not the only cause of nitrate pollution. When cattle and pigs are reared intensively, they spend nearly all their lives indoors. Their waste products are collected as thick, liquid slurry. It is used as fertilizer, where it can be washed off by rain into nearby streams or ground-water supplies.

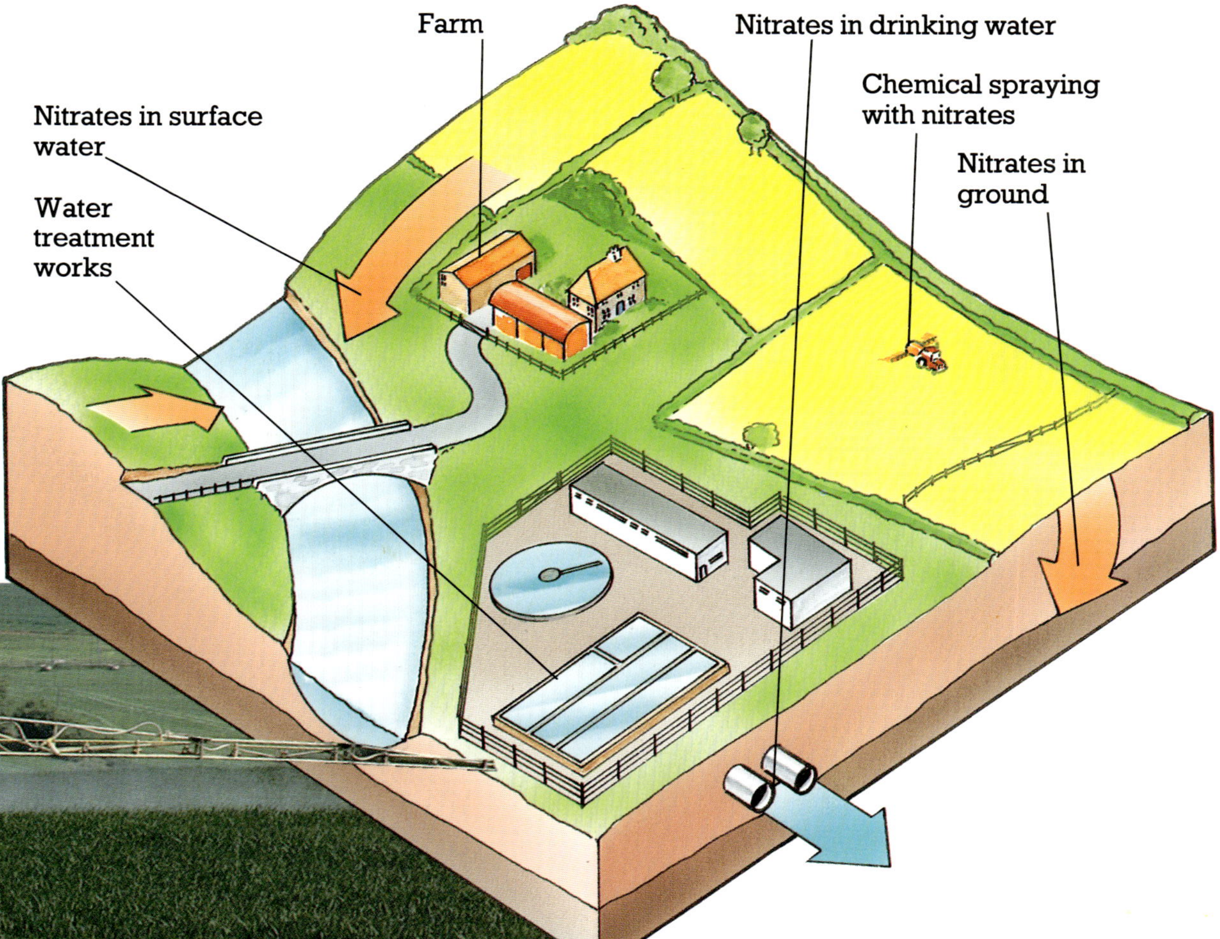

FARMING FACTS

Although many go hungry, the world actually grows enough food. The 2 billion tonnes of staple crops we produce could feed another 1.5 billion people. But a lot of our cereal production goes into animal feed in order to supply the developed countries with a meat-rich diet.

Only about 10 per cent of the land surface is suitable for agriculture, and most of our food comes from intensive farming. Shifting cultivation and nomadic pastoralism contribute little to the global larder. Intensive cultivation either requires a great deal of labour or masses of machines. Today, both approaches rely on the extensive use of pesticides and fertilizer.

Much of the money spent on research goes into devising new weapons to fight species that have developed resistance to existing pesticides. As the number of resistant species increases, so does the money spent on research. Genetic engineering offers new opportunities for the future, but there is concern about further "tinkering" with nature.

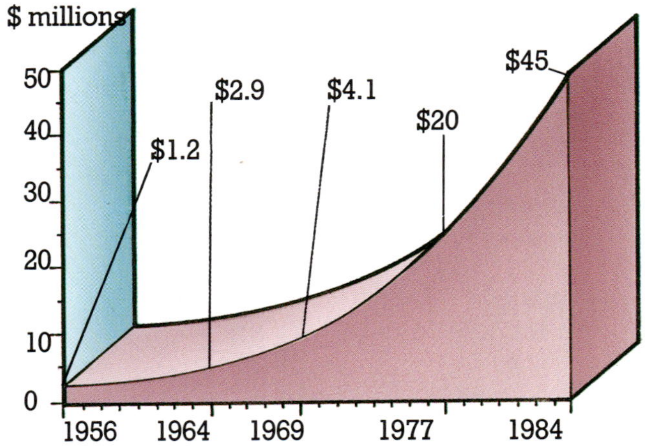

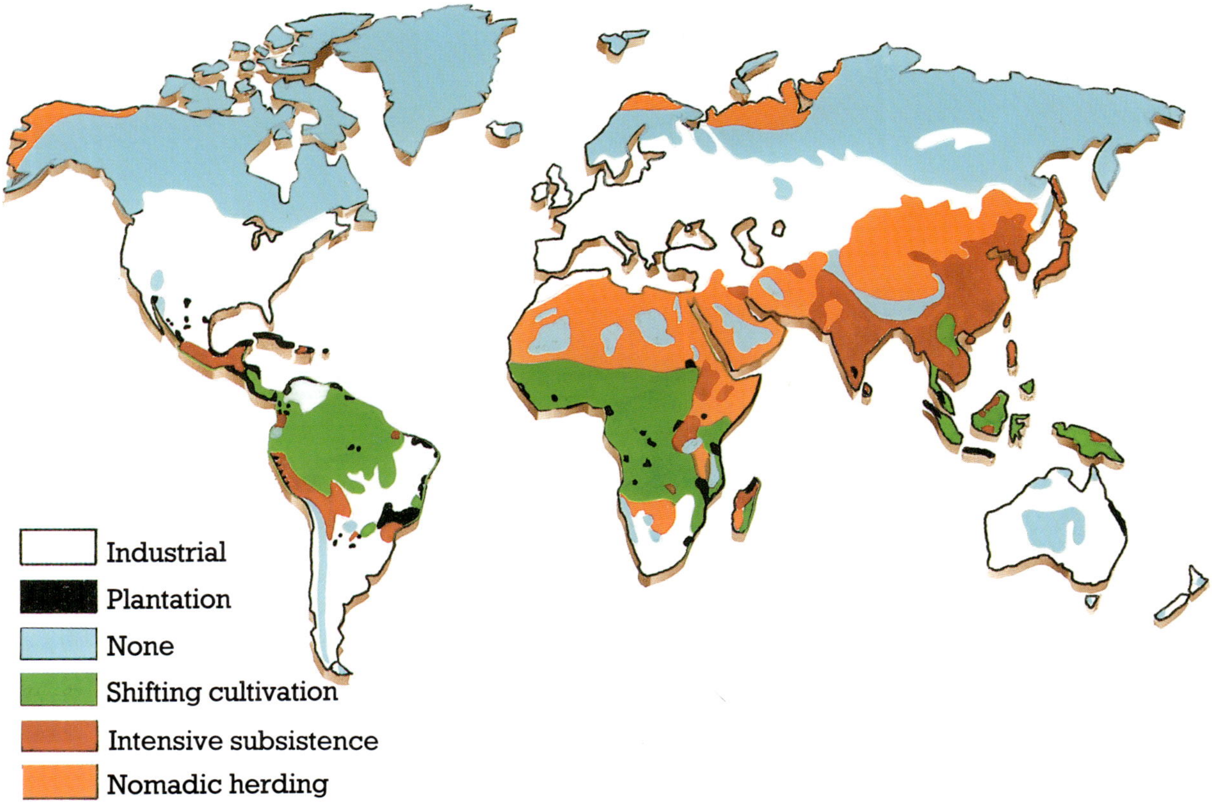

GLOSSARY

agriculture – any type of farming whether crops or animals, mechanised or not.

compost – lawn-clippings, leaves, and other organic solid waste which has been broken down by bacteria to produce a humus-like substance which can be used as a fertilizer.

DDT (Dichlorodiphenyl-trichloroethane) – a persistent pesticide.

ecosystem – self-regulating natural community of plants and animals interacting with themselves and with their environment.

epidemic – widespread outbreak of an infectious disease. Transmission by pest carriers frequently starts epidemics.

fertilizer – plant food, anything that is added to the soil in order to increase its fertility.

hormones – chemical messengers that travel around an organism's body in the sap or bloodstream.

plague – usually means the disease bubonic plague. It is often used to refer to any sudden and large-scale attack by a pest.

resistance – degree of immunity to a particular drug or chemical. Some species have natural resistance to particular substances. Some, especially bacteria, can develop resistance in as little as a few months. Insects can develop resistance in four years.

USEFUL ADDRESSES

Friends of the Earth has over 220 local groups and some 20,000 supporters throughout Britain who may be able to help you. FoE campaigns for the environment and takes a strong stand against pollution. Information is available from Friends of the Earth, 26-27 Underwood St, London N1 7JQ.

Greenpeace is an international organisation dedicated to protecting the environment. It makes peaceful protests in order to make the public aware of what it considers the worst problems. Information is available from Greenpeace, 30-31 Islington Green, London N1 8XE.

The Council for the Protection of Rural England actively campaigns on a local and national level to protect the British countryside. Their headquarters is at 4 Hobart Place, London SW1W OHY.

The Green Party The "Greens", as they are often called, are the political party dedicated to the environment. They supply information packs for schools as well as other useful information. Contact The Green Party, 10 Station Parade, Balham High St, London SW12.

INDEX

PRINTED IN BELGIUM BY proost INTERNATIONAL BOOK PRODUCTION